WEBER'S
Fun & Easy
Grilling
Guide™

WEBER'S®
Fun & Easy
Grilling Guide™

SIMPLE BARBECUE BASICS

LUCY KNOX

MQP

Published by MQ Publications Limited
12 The Ivories, 6–8 Northampton Street
London N1 2HY
Tel: 44 (0)20 7359 2244
Fax: 44 (0)20 7359 1616
email: mail@mqpublications.com
www.mqpublications.com

Produced by MQ Publications Ltd under
exclusive licence from Weber-Stephen
Products Co.

MQ Publications:
Zaro Weil, CEO & Publisher

Weber-Stephen Products Co.:
Mike Kempster Sr., Executive Vice President
Jeff Stephen, Vice President Export Sales

Photography: Gareth Sambidge
Home Economy: Caroline Marson
Styling: Penny Markham
Recipe Credits: Lucy Knox

ISBN: 1-84072-789-6

1 3 5 7 9 0 8 6 4 2

Printed and bound in France by *Partenaires-Livres*®.

Introduction

Nothing beats a good barbecue. It's not really surprising. We have been cooking over open fires since the dawn of time. The word barbecue comes from the Spanish 'barbacoa' meaning a structure on which meat can be dried or roasted.

Sales of barbecues as we know them – designed for families to cook in backyards and gardens – exploded in the second half of the 20th century. They have always been popular in Australia and South Africa and countries in the Americas where the climate is suited to outdoor entertaining. The dimensions of the barbecue experience have expanded and thanks to the unique design of Weber® grills we can enjoy cooking in less than perfect weather.

Barbecues mean less fuss, less fat, more flavour and more fun. Good company and good conversation are enjoyed as great food sizzles and smokes on the barbie. I grew up in the countryside outside London and remember with great affection the brilliant family barbecues my parents used to do every summer. And now my husband and I love nothing more than cooking with our two little girls for friends whenever we can. It's such a wonderful way to cook – and to entertain!

Barbecuing spells ease, so look for the shortcuts that leave you more time for conversation and recreation. Buying your salads ready washed and ready prepared will save you a huge amount of time, for example.

If you are new to the world of barbecuing be sure to spend time reading the barbecue techniques section at the beginning of the book. This section is jam-packed with barbecue tips, cooking charts and shortcuts that even the seasoned griller will find useful.

Dip in and out of this useful, easy-to-follow chapter as and when you need to. Extensive time charts for a wide variety of ingredients are included – use these charts when you are experimenting with the recipes included and attempting to try something new – they will act as a useful guideline to creating the perfect barbecue results.

As well as barbecue techniques you'll find invaluable hints and tips on barbecue safety. This includes the ideal positioning of the barbecue for safe grilling and the safest barbecue tools to use, eliminating flare-ups whilst cooking and information on keeping food hygiene levels at a high at all times.

The dishes in this book are designed to be quick and easy: simple yet stylish; perfect for effortless entertaining in gardens, backyards, balconies or beaches. Above all, these Weber barbecue dishes are absolutely delicious. Just right for anyone who loves cooking – and eating – great barbecue food!

Barbecue Basics

CHARCOAL GRILLS

The secret of cooking on a charcoal kettle lies in the proper use of the lid and the vent system, along with two proven methods of positioning the charcoal briquettes. Air is drawn through the bottom vents to provide the oxygen necessary to keep the coals burning. The air heats and rises and is reflected off the lid, so it circulates around the food being cooked, eventually passing out through the top vent.

The art of charcoal barbecuing lies in mastering the fire – knowing how to set it up and how to control the temperature. Once you master that, it's easy and fun to cook entire menus and experiment with different combinations – and when you get the timing right, your guests will be able to enjoy all the food hot from the barbecue at the right time!

BUILDING THE FIRE

- **Use the right fuel:** solid hardwood charcoal briquettes are best. Look for either the square or round (also known as beads) types. Stay away from petroleum-based charcoal briquettes. They may last longer but they give off an unpleasant taste.

- **Use firelighters:** the waxy looking sticks or cubes – whenever possible, as they do not impart the chemical flavour often found when using lighter fluids. Firelighters also burn in all types of weather, ensuring a fast start to the fire. (If using lighter fluid, use it only on dry coals – never spray it on a lit fire!)

TIP

Always keep vents open. The wider the vent opening, the hotter the fire. At all times, remember to sweep ashes regularly so that the bottom vent stays clear.

LIGHTING YOUR GRILL

1. Remove the lid and open all of the air vents before building the fire. Spread the charcoal over the charcoal grate to determine how much you will need, then pile it into a mound in the centre of the grate.

2. Insert 4 firelighters (see *figure 1*), light them and let the coals catch alight and burn (see *figure 2*) until they are covered with a light grey ash. This usually takes about 20 to 25 minutes. You can also use a chimney starter (see the note on page 11).

3. Use tongs to arrange the coals on the grate according to the cooking method you are going to use.

- **For Direct cooking** (see *figure 3* and page 16), you should have an even layer of hot coals across the charcoal grate.

- **For Indirect cooking** (see *figure 4* and page 17), you should have enough coals to arrange them evenly on either side of the charcoal grate.

4. Finally, place the cooking grate over the coals, put the lid on and preheat the cooking grate for about 10 minutes. The grill is now ready to use.

figure 1

figure 2

figure 3

figure 4

HOW MUCH FUEL IS RIGHT?

Use the following charts for your initial settings, depending on the size of your barbecue. The best way to control the temperature of the barbecue is to adjust the number of coals. To get a hotter fire, add more coals to your initial settings. For a lower temperature, use fewer coals. This may require a little experimentation on your part, but eventually you will know what's right for your barbecue and the foods that you cook most often.

How many briquettes you need to use

BBQ kettle	Square traditional briquettes	Round charcoal beads
37cm diameter	15 each side	12–24 each side
47cm diameter	20 each side	28–56 each side
57cm diameter	25 each side	44–88 each side
95cm diameter	75 each side	4–8kg each side
Charcoal Go-Anywhere®	10 each side	12–24 each side

How many briquettes you need to add per hour for Indirect cooking

BBQ kettle	Number of coals per side / per hour
37cm diameter	6
47cm diameter	7
57cm diameter	8
95cm diameter	22
Charcoal Go-Anywhere®	6

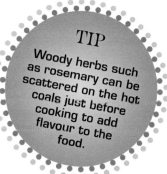

TIP

Woody herbs such as rosemary can be scattered on the hot coals just before cooking to add flavour to the food.

LIGHTING AGENTS

• **Firelighters:** Barbecue firelighters are waxy looking cubes or sticks, which are designed to light the barbecue without giving off any harmful fumes that could taint the food. Push four into the charcoal and light with a taper or a long stem match. They are easy to use, clean and safe. Only use firelighters designed for barbecues. Do not use firelighters designed for domestic fires as they contain paraffin, which will spoil the food.

• **Firelighter fluid:** If using this product you should handle with care. It should be sprayed on the dry coals, left for a few minutes to soak in, then ignited with a taper or long stem match. Never spray on hot or burning coals because the flames can travel up into the bottle causing serious burns.

CHIMNEY STARTER

A metal canister with a handle, a chimney starter holds a supply of charcoal. Crumpled newspaper or firelighters are put on the charcoal grate and lit, the chimney starter filled with coals is positioned over the firelighters. The walls of the chimney starter focus the flames and heat onto the charcoal, decreasing the amount of time it takes for the coals to light and ash over. Once the coals are ready, simply tip the coals onto the charcoal grate and arrange them for barbecuing.

EXTINGUISHING THE FIRE

1. Before you extinguish the coals, remove all food from the cooking grate and replace the lid. Allow the barbecue to continue heating the cooking grate until any smoking stops, 10 to 15 minutes, to burn off any cooking residues. Then give the grate a good brushing with a brass-bristle brush.

2. Close the lid and all the vents and let the barbecue cool down.

3. Do not handle hot ashes. Wait until they are cold, and remove them so they don't attract moisture and encourage rust. Some grills are equipped with blades that sweep the ashes into ash pans or catchers. Dispose of the ashes properly in a fireproof container. Always remove the ashes before storing a charcoal barbecue.

GAS GRILLS

Gas grills have one main advantage over charcoal and that's speed. Push the ignition switch and within about 10 minutes the barbecue is up to heat and ready to use. The workings of a gas barbecue are simple. First come burners to create heat, then some type of system above the burners to help disperse the heat, such as metal bars, lava rocks, or ceramic briquettes. Above this is the cooking grate. Underneath the cooking box is a tray for collecting debris and fats.

Gas barbecues are run on Liquid Petroleum (LP) gas, which comes in two forms, butane or propane. The gas is under moderate pressure in the cylinder and is liquid. As the pressure is released the liquid vaporizes and becomes a gas.

LIGHTING YOUR GRILL

1. Check that there is enough fuel in your gas bottle (some barbecues have gauges to measure how much is left) and make sure that the burner control knobs are turned off.

2. Open the lid. Turn the gas valve on the bottle to 'on'.

3. Turn on the starter burner and light the grill according to the manufacturer's instructions using either the ignition switch or a match. When the gas flame has ignited, turn on the other burners.

4. Close the lid and preheat the grill until the thermometer reads 245 to 275°C. This takes about 10 minutes.

5. Using a brass bristle brush, clean the grate to remove any debris left over from your last barbecue.

TIP

Always read the safety instructions carefully on transporting, storing and fitting gas bottles.

6. Adjust the burner controls according to the cooking method, Direct (*figure 5*) or Indirect (*figure 6*), you are going to use. The barbecue is now ready for cooking.

figure 5   *figure 6*

GETTING THE RIGHT TEMPERATURE

Most gas barbecues today have burner controls that are set to Low, Medium and High, but each model uses a different temperature, so be sure to learn what those are on your model. The recipes in this book are gauged to temperatures of about 150°C for Low; 180°C for Medium; and 245 to 275°C for High. Some gas barbecues have a built-in thermometer, but if yours does not, use an oven thermometer placed on the cooking grate.

TURNING THE FIRE OFF

1. Make sure all burners are switched to 'off'. Then, shut the gas down at the source.

2. When the barbecue has cooled down, preferably the next day, remove the catch pan from the bottom tray, or empty the drip tray so you don't get flare-ups or grease fires the next time you barbecue.

SMOKING

It's easy to add a more distinctive flavour to barbecued food by adding manufactured or natural flavourings to the smouldering coals, or the smoker box in the case of gas barbecues, before cooking. There are many types of flavoured woods and herbs available. They come in either chunks or chips, and should be soaked in cold water for at least 30 minutes prior to use.

● **On a charcoal barbecue:** Place the soaked chunks, chips or herbs directly on the hot coals. Add the food to the cooking grate and barbecue according to the recipe.

● **On a gas barbecue:** If your barbecue has a smoker box accessory, follow the manufacturer's instructions. If your barbecue does not have a smoker box accessory, simply place the chunks, chips or herbs in a small metal foil pan, cover with aluminium foil (poke holes in the aluminium foil to allow smoke to escape) and place directly over the heat disbursement system or the cooking grate in one corner. Turn the grill on and, as it heats up, smoke will begin to form, and will flavour the food as it cooks. Never place the food directly over the pan of smoking materials.

weber ♀ AND weber baby ♀

The Weber® Q™ is the first gas barbecue that can act as both a fully functioning barbecue for your garden and a portable gas barbecue.

Compact, just 46cm from front to back, and 80cm from handle to handle, the porcelain-enamelled cast-iron cooking grate lets you grill up to 10 king-size steaks or 15 burgers at the same time and a deep lid can cover a whole chicken.

The Weber® Q™ and Weber® Baby Q™ (see *figure 7* and picture opposite) work in much the same way as other Weber gas barbecues with the exception that you cannot cook using the Indirect method on these grills. You can achieve a similar result by reducing the temperature to low and cooking larger cuts of meat on a roast holder. Where the cooking times and methods differ slightly than normal these are noted on the grilling charts on pages 22–27 and in the grilling methods noted at the start of each recipe.

figure 7

TIP

Remember, never store your barbecue indoors with the bottle attached. If properly covered, a gas barbecue can withstand the elements outside and always be ready for action.

LIGHTING WEBER® Q™ BARBECUES

1. Check that there is enough fuel in your gas bottle and that the burner control knob is turned off.

2. Open the lid and, on the Weber® Q™ gas grill, unfold the side tables.

3. Set the burner control knob to START/HI. Press the red igniter button to light the grill.

4. Close the lid and preheat the grill for about 10 minutes. The temperature will probably have reached approximately 245 to 275°C by this point.

5. Adjust the burner control knob according to the cooking method you are going to use.

EXTINGUISHING THE FIRE

1. To clean your cooking grate turn the burner to HI and leave for about 10 minutes. Then brush the cooking grate with a brass-bristle brush.

2. Make sure the burner is switched to 'off'. Then, shut the gas down at the source.

3. When the barbecue has cooled down, preferably the next day, remove the catch pan from the bottom tray, or empty the drip tray so you don't get flare-ups or grease fires the next time you barbecue.

DIRECT COOKING

The Direct method means that the food is cooked directly over the heat source. To ensure that foods cook evenly, turn them only once, halfway through the grilling time. Direct cooking is also the best technique for searing meats. In addition to creating a wonderful caramelized texture and flavour, searing also adds grill marks to the surface of the meat. To sear meats, place them over Direct heat for 2 to 5 minutes per side. Remember that smaller pieces of meat require less searing time, and be especially mindful of too much searing on very lean cuts of meat as they can dry out quickly. After searing, finish cooking using the method called for in the recipe.

ON CHARCOAL

1. Prepare and light the coals as instructed on pages 8 to 9. Remember, don't begin to barbecue until the coals are covered in a light grey ash. Spread the prepared coals in an even layer across the charcoal grate.

2. Set the cooking grate over the coals, put the lid on and preheat the cooking grate for about 10 minutes. Place the food on the cooking grate and cover with the lid. The food will cook directly over the heat source (see *figure 8*).

3. Do not lift the lid during cooking time, except to turn the food once halfway through and to test for readiness.

figure 8

ON GAS

1. To set up the barbecue for Direct cooking, first preheat with all burners on High. Once the barbecue is up to heat, usually about 10 minutes, adjust all burners to the temperature called for in the recipe.

2. Place the food on the cooking grate over and close the lid. Again, the food will be cooked over the heat source (see *figure 9*).

3. Do not lift the lid during cooking time, except to turn the food once halfway through and to test for readiness.

figure 9

INDIRECT COOKING

Indirect cooking is similar to roasting, but the barbecue adds flavour and texture that you can't get from the oven. The heat rises and reflects off the lid and inside surfaces of the barbecue to cook the food slowly and evenly on all sides. As in a convection oven, there is no need to turn the food over because the heat circulates around the food.

ON CHARCOAL

1. Prepare and light the coals as instructed on pages 8 to 9. Remember, don't begin to barbecue until the coals are covered in a light grey ash. Arrange the hot coals evenly on either side of the charcoal grate. Charcoal/fuel baskets or rails are accessories that keep the coals in place.

2. Place a drip pan in the centre of the charcoal grate between the coals to catch drippings. The drip pan also helps prevent flare-ups when cooking fatty foods such as duck, goose or fatty roasts. For longer cooking times, add water to the drip pan to keep the fat and food particles from burning.

3. Set the cooking grate over the coals, put the lid on and preheat the cooking grate for about 10 minutes. Place the food on the cooking grate over the drip pan and between the heat zones above the coals (see *figure 10*).

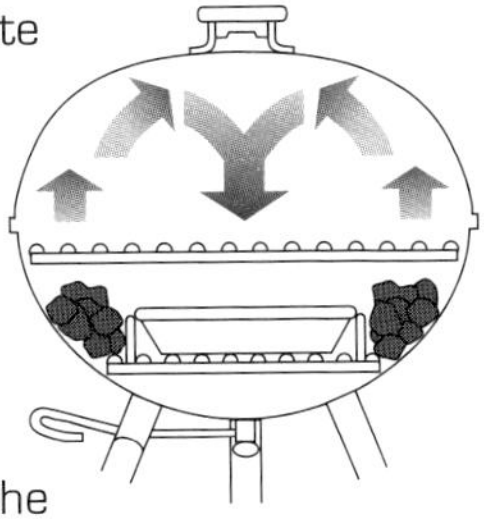

figure 10

4. Close the lid and open it only to add coals for longer cooking times, baste the meat or check for readiness.

ON GAS

1. Preheat the barbecue with all burners on High. Once the barbecue is up to heat, usually about 10 minutes, adjust the burners to the temperature called for in the recipe, turning off the burner(s) directly below the food.

2. Place the food on the cooking grate between the heat zones (see *figure 11*). For best results with roasts, poultry or large cuts of meat, use a roasting rack set inside a metal foil pan to catch the drippings.

3. Close the lid and open it only to baste the meat or check for readiness.

figure 11

17

BARBECUE HINTS AND TIPS

- **Stating the Obvious**
  Always make sure the barbecue is up to temperature before beginning to cook. For charcoal grilling, the charcoal should have a light grey ash on it for a good hot fire, which takes between 25 and 30 minutes. Use a chimney starter for best results. For gas grilling, first, open the lid (unfold the work surfaces on the Q™ gas grill), turn on the gas source, turn the burner control knobs to High (START/HI on the Q™ gas grill) and push a button to ignite the burner(s). Shut the lid, leave for about 10 minutes and you're ready to barbecue.

- **Down, Boy**
  Always cook with the lid of your barbecue down or on. This will reduce the chances of flare-ups and cook your food faster and more evenly. While cooking, resist the urge to open the lid to check on your dinner every couple of minutes. Every time you lift the lid, heat escapes causing your food to take longer to cook.

- **Don't Flip Out**
  Unless the recipe calls for it, flip your food just once.

- **Easy on the Squeeze**
  Resist the urge to use your spatula to press down on foods such as burgers or steaks. In doing this you'll only succeed in squeezing out all of the flavour, not making it cook faster.

- **Moisturize**
  A light coating of oil will help brown your food evenly and keep it from sticking to the cooking grate. Always brush or spray oil on your food, not the cooking grate.

- **Forego the Fork**
  Poking meat with a fork whilst cooking causes juices and flavour to escape and dries out your food. Just use the fork for lifting food from the grill and nothing more.

- **Cut It Out**
  Trim excess fat from steaks, chops, and roasts leaving no more than a scant 5mm thick layer.

- **Adjust to Your Environment**
  Grilling times listed in the recipes are approximate. Allow more time on cold or windy days or at higher altitudes.

- **Procrastinate**
  When using a marinade or glaze with a high sugar content or other ingredients that burn easily, brush on food only during the last 10 to 15 minutes of cooking.

- **Is Dinner Ready Yet?**
  A kitchen timer and an instant-read

thermometer are your best defenses against overcooked foods. Use the thermometer to check on readiness in roasts, or thick cuts of meat, but never leave it in the food while cooking.

- **Every Time You Grill**
  Do the burn off. On a gas grill, turn all of the burners on high, close the lid, leave for about 10 to 15 minutes, then brush the cooking grates thoroughly with a brass-bristle, long-handled grill brush (use a steel brush on cast-iron grates). For a charcoal grill, unless you have a very hot fire going when you are finished barbecuing, it's easier to clean your cooking grate right before you begin cooking – after the grate has pre-heated.

SAFE SIZZLE

- Always keep the barbecue at least 3m away from any combustible materials including the house, garage and fences.

- Do not use the grill indoors or under a covered patio, open garage door or carport.

- Keep children and pets away from a hot barbecue at all times.

- Do not add lighter fluid to a lit fire.

- Make sure the barbecue is sturdy; do not use if it wobbles, or is otherwise unstable. Always stand the barbecue on a level surface.

- Use heat-resistant barbecue mitts and long-handled tongs to turn the food.

- Do not spray oil on a hot cooking grate; oil the food instead.

- Do not use water to extinguish a flare-up. Close the lid (and all vents on a charcoal grill) to reduce the oxygen flow and eliminate flare-ups. If necessary, turn a gas grill off at the source. Keep a fire extinguisher handy in case of a mishap.

- Do not store propane tanks indoors or in the garage.

- Do not line the bottom of a barbecue or cover the cooking grate with foil. This obstructs airflow and also collects grease, which can result in flare-ups.

- When finished barbecuing, close the lid and all vents on a charcoal barbecue; close the lid and turn off all burners and the LP tank or source on a gas grill. Make sure that hot coals are fully extinguished before leaving the barbecue site.

FOOD SAFETY

● Defrost meat, fish and poultry only in the refrigerator, never at room temperature.

● Allow meats to come to room temperature before cooking, but do not do so in a room that is over 21°C. Do not place raw food in direct sunlight or near a heat source.

● When using a sauce during barbecuing, divide it in half and keep one part separate for serving with the finished dish. Use the other half for basting the meat; do not use this as a sauce for serving. If using a marinade that was used on raw meats, fish or poultry, boil it vigorously for at least 1 full minute before using it as a baste or sauce.

● Do not place cooked food on the same dish that the raw food was placed on prior to cooking.

● Wash all dishes, plates, cooking utensils, barbecuing tools and work surfaces that have come into contact with raw meats or fish with hot soapy water. Wash your hands thoroughly after handling raw meats or fish.

● Chill any leftover cooked food from the barbecue once it has cooled.

● Always barbecue minced meats to at least 71°C (77°C for poultry), the temperature for medium (well-done) readiness.

ACCESSORIES

For best results, use the right tools when barbecuing. Here is a list of some of the essentials:

● Wide metal spatula – used for turning chicken pieces, vegetables and smaller pieces of food.

● Long-handled grill brush – preferably with brass bristles, to keep the grates clean without scratching the porcelain enamel. A steel-bristle brush is best for cleaning cast-iron grates.

● Basting brush – used for basting food with marinade or oil. Best with natural bristles (nylon bristles will melt if they touch the cooking grate) and a long handle.

● Long-handled tongs – used for turning sausages, shellfish, kebabs, etc.

● Long-handled fork – used for lifting cooked roasts and whole poultry from the barbecue.

● Barbecue mitts/oven gloves – these should be long-sleeved, flame-resistant gloves to protect your hands and forearms.

● Skewers – wooden or metal skewers are excellent for holding small pieces of meat, fish or vegetables and make it easy to turn food quickly on the barbecue, ensuring faster cooking. Remember to soak wooden

skewers, if using them, in cold water for at least 30 minutes before adding the food.

● Meat thermometer – used for best results every time, a thermometer takes the guess work out of judging if food is cooked.

● Timer – an excellent tool, so you don't have to watch the clock and can continue preparing other parts of the meal while the food is cooking.

● Foil drip pans – these keep the base of the barbecue clean and gather fats and juices that fall from the food during cooking.

● Roast holder – when cooking large cuts of meat and poultry on a gas barbecue, a roast holder in a foil pan will catch the drippings and reduce the chance of flare-ups.

TIP

Long-handled equipment not only makes the job safer but also quicker and more efficient.

BARBECUE GUIDES

The following thicknesses, weights and barbecue times are meant to be general guidelines rather than firm rules and you may notice that recipe times vary in comparison. When following a recipe, always follow the specific instructions. Cooking times are affected by wind, outside temperature and desired degree of cooking.

KEY TO METHOD OF COOKING

In the following fish, meat, poultry, vegetable and fruit cooking charts the approximate cooking time is followed by the barbecue method. These methods are also referred to throughout the book. Note: when cooking on Weber® Q™ or Baby Q™ always turn food once halfway through cooking, even if using a roast holder.

DL	Direct Low Heat
DM	Direct Medium Heat
DH	Direct High Heat
IL	Indirect Low Heat
IM	Indirect Medium Heat
IH	Indirect High Heat

Fish & Seafood	Thickness/Weight	Grilling Time for Gas/Charcoal	Grilling Time for Weber® Q™ and Baby Q™
Fish fillet or steak	5mm to 1cm thick	3 to 5 minutes DH	3 to 5 minutes DH
	1 to 2.5cm thick	5 to 10 minutes DH	5 to 10 minutes DH
	2.5 to 3cm thick	10 to 12 minutes DH	10 to 12 minutes DH
Fish, whole	450g	15 to 20 minutes IM	15 to 20 minutes DM
	900 to 1.1kg	20 to 30 minutes IM	20 to 30 minutes DM
	1.4kg	30 to 45 minutes IM	
Fish kebab	2.5cm thick	8 to 10 minutes DM	8 to 10 minutes DM
Prawn		2 to 4 minutes DH	2 to 4 minutes DH
Scallop		3 to 6 minutes DH	3 to 6 minutes DH
Mussel		5 to 6 minutes DH	5 to 6 minutes DH
(discard any that do not open)			
Clam		8 to 10 minutes DH	8 to 10 minutes DH
(discard any that do not open)			
Oyster		3 to 5 minutes DH	3 to 5 minutes DH
Lobster tail		7 to 11 minutes DM	7 to 11 minutes DM

Note: General rule for grilling fish: 4 to 5 minutes per 1cm thickness; 8 to 10 minutes per 2.5cm thickness.

Beef	Thickness/Weight	Grilling Time for Gas/Charcoal	Grilling Time for Weber® Q™ and Baby Q™
Steak: sirloin, T-bone or rib	2.5cm thick	6 to 8 minutes DH	6 to 8 minutes DH
	3cm thick	8 to 10 minutes DH	8 to 10 minutes DH
	4cm thick	12 to 16 minutes total; sear 8 to 10 minutes cook 4 to 6 minutes IH	12 to 16 minutes total; sear 8 to 10 minutes DH, cook 4 to 6 minutes DL
	5cm thick	18 to 22 minutes total; sear 8 to 10 minutes DH, cook 10 to 12 minutes IH	
Skirt steak	5mm to 1cm thick	4 to 6 minutes DH	4 to 6 minutes DH
Flank steak	650 to 900g 2cm thick	8 to 10 minutes DH	8 to 10 minutes DH
Kebab	2.5 to 4cm cubes	7 to 8 minutes DH	7 to 8 minutes DH
Tenderloin, whole	1.5 to 1.75kg	35 to 50 minutes total; sear 15 minutes DM, cook 20 to 30 minutes IM	45 to 50 minutes (medium rare); sear 12 minutes DH (turn 4 times), cook 33 to 38 minutes DL
Minced beef burger	2cm thick	8 to 10 minutes DH	8 to 10 minutes DM
Rib roast (prime rib), boneless	2.25kg to 2.75kg	1¼ to 1¾ hours IM	1½ to 2 hours DL (on roasting rack) – on Q™ grill only
Strip loin roast, boneless	1.75kg to 2.25kg	45 to 60 minutes total; sear 2 to 4 minutes DH, cook 45 to 60 minutes IM	
Veal loin chop	2.5cm thick	6 to 8 minutes DH	6 to 8 minutes DH

Note: All cooking times are for medium-rare readiness, except ground beef and ground lamb (medium).

Safe Cooking Temperature for Beef

Cook beef roasts and steaks to 62°C for medium rare (71°C for medium) / cook minced beef to at least 71°C.

Pork	Thickness/Weight	Grilling Time for Gas/Charcoal	Grilling Time for Weber® Q™ and Baby Q™
Bratwurst, fresh		20 to 25 minutes DM	25 to 30 minutes DL
Bratwurst, pre-cooked		10 to 12 minutes DM	10 to 12 minutes DM
Pork chop, boneless or	1cm thick	5 to 7 minutes DH	5 to 8 minutes DH
bone-in	2cm thick	6 to 8 minutes DH	
	2.5cm thick	8 to 10 minutes DM	8 to 10 minutes DM
	3 to 4cm thick	10 to 12 minutes total; sear 6 minutes DH, cook 4 to 6 minutes IM	14 to 18 minutes total; sear 8 minutes DH, cook 6 to 10 minutes DL
Loin roast, boneless	1kg	40 to 45 minutes DM	
Loin roast, bone-in	1.25 to 2.25kg	$1^{1}/_{4}$ to $1^{3}/_{4}$ hours IM	$1^{1}/_{4}$ to $1^{3}/_{4}$ hours DL (on roasting rack) – on Q™ only
Pork shoulder, boneless	2.25 to to 2.75kg	$3^{1}/_{2}$ to 4 hours DL	
Pork, minced	2cm thick	8 to 10 minutes DM	8 to 10 minutes DM
Ribs, baby back	700 to 900g	$1^{1}/_{2}$ to 2 hours IL	See directly below
Ribs, spareribs	1.25 to 2.25kg	$2^{1}/_{2}$ to 3 hours IL	$1^{1}/_{4}$ to $1^{1}/_{2}$ hours DL (on rib rack) – on Q™ only
Ribs, country-style, boneless	700 to 900g	12 to 15 minutes DM	
Ribs, country-style	1.25 to 1.75kg	$1^{1}/_{2}$ to 2 hours IM	
Tenderloin, whole	350 to 450g	15 to 20 minutes DM	25 to 30 minutes total; sear 10 minutes DH (turn 3 times), then cook 15 to 20 minutes DL

Safe Cooking Temperature for Pork
Cook all pork to 71°C.

Safe Cooking Temperature for Lamb
Cook lamb to 62°C for medium rare (71°C for medium) / cook minced lamb to 71°C.

Safe Cooking Temperature for Poultry
Cook whole poultry to 82°C / cook minced poultry to 74°C / cook chicken breasts to 77°C / cook duck and goose to 82°C.

Lamb	Thickness/Weight	Grilling Time for Gas/Charcoal	Grilling Time for Weber® Q™ and Baby Q™
Chop: loin, rib, shoulder, or sirloin	2cm to 3cm thick	8 to 12 minutes DM	8 to 12 minutes DM
Leg of lamb roast,	2.25 to 3.25kg	$1^1/_4$ to $1^3/_4$ hours IM	2 to $2^1/_2$ boneless hours DL (on roasting rack) – Q™ only
Leg of lamb, butterflied	1.25 to 1.5kg	$1^1/_4$ to $1^1/_2$ hours total; sear 10 to 15 minutes DM, cook 1 to $1^1/_4$ hours IM	
Rib crown roast	1.25 to 1.75kg	1 to $1^1/_4$ hours IM	
Minced lamb burger	2cm thick	8 to 10 minutes DM	8 to 10 minutes DM
Rack of lamb	450 to 700g	20 to 30 minutes DM	20 to 30 minutes DM

Note: All cooking times are for medium-rare readiness, except ground beef and ground lamb (medium).

Poultry	Thickness/Weight	Grilling Time for Gas/Charcoal	Grilling Time for Weber® Q™ and Baby Q™
Chicken breast, boneless, skinless	175g	8 to 12 minutes DM	8 to 12 minutes DM
Chicken thigh, boneless, skinless	115g	8 to 10 minutes DH	8 to 10 minutes DH
Chicken pieces, bone-in breast/wing		30 to 40 minutes IM	30 to 40 minutes DL
Chicken pieces, bone-in leg/thigh		40 to 50 minutes IM	40 to 50 minutes DL
Chicken, whole	1.5 to 2.25kg	1 to $1^1/_2$ hours IM	1 to $1^1/_2$ hours DL (on roasting rack) – on Q™ grill only
Chicken kebab	2.5cm thick	6 to 8 minutes DM	6 to 8 minutes DM
Cornish game hen	700 to 900g	30 to 45 minutes IM	30 to 35 minutes DL
Turkey breast, boneless	1.25kg	1 to $1^1/_4$ hours IM	
Turkey, whole, unstuffed	4.5 to 5kg	$1^3/_4$ to $2^1/_2$ hours IM	
	5.5 to 6.5kg	$2^1/_4$ to 3 hours IM	
	6.75 to 7.75kg	$2^3/_4$ to $3^3/_4$ hours IM	
	8 to 10kg	$3^1/_2$ to 4 hours IM	
Duck breast, boneless	200 to 225g	12 to 15 minutes DL	12 to 15 minutes DL
Duck, whole	2.25 to 2.75kg	40 minutes IH	

Vegetables	Grilling Time for Gas/Charcoal	Grilling Time for Weber® Q™ and Baby Q™
Artichoke, whole	boil 12 to 15 minutes; cut in half and grill 4 to 6 minutes DM	boil 12 to 15 minutes; cut in half and grill 4 to 6 minutes DM
Asparagus	6 to 8 minutes DM	6 to 8 minutes DM
Aubergine, 1cm slices	8 to 10 minutes DM	8 to 10 minutes DM
Aubergine, halved	12 to 15 minutes DM	12 to 15 minutes DM
Beet	1 to 1$\frac{1}{2}$ hours IM	1 to 1$\frac{1}{2}$ hours DL
Corn, husked	10 to 15 minutes DM	10 to 12 minutes DM
Corn, in husk	25 to 30 minutes DM	25 to 30 minutes DM
Courgette, 1cm slices	6 to 8 minutes DM	6 to 8 minutes DM
Courgette, halved	6 to 10 minutes DM	6 to 10 minutes DM
Fennel, 5mm slices	10 to 12 minutes DM	10 to 12 minutes DM
Garlic, whole	45 to 60 minutes IM	45 to 60 minutes DL
Green bean, whole	8 to 10 minutes DM	8 to 10 minutes DM
Green onion, whole	3 to 4 minutes DM	3 to 4 minutes DM
Leek, halved	steam 4 to 5 minutes; grill 3 to 5 minutes DM	steam 4 to 5 minutes; grill 3 to 5 minutes DM
Mushroom: shiitake or button	8 to 10 minutes DM	8 to 10 minutes DM
Mushroom: portabello	10 to 15 minutes DM	12 to 15 minutes DM
Onion, halved	35 to 40 minutes IM	
Onion, 1cm slices	8 to 12 minutes DM	8 to 12 minutes DM
pepper, whole	10 to 15 minutes DM	10 to 12 minutes DM
pepper, 5mm slices	6 to 8 minutes DM	6 to 8 minutes DM
Potato, whole	45 to 60 minutes IM	45 to 60 minutes DL
Potato, 1cm slices	14 to 16 minutes DM	14 to 16 minutes DM
Potato: new, halved	15 to 20 minutes DM	15 to 20 minutes DM
Pumpkin (1.25kg), halved	1$\frac{1}{2}$ to 2 hours IM	1$\frac{1}{2}$ to 2 hours DL
Squash: acorn (450g), halved	1 to 1$\frac{1}{4}$ hours IM	1 to 1$\frac{1}{4}$ hours DL
Squash: butternut (900g), halved	50 to 55 minutes IM	50 to 55 minutes DL
Squash: patty pan	10 to 12 minutes DM	10 to 12 minutes DM
Squash: yellow, 1cm slices	6 to 8 minutes DM	6 to 8 minutes DM
Squash: yellow, halved	6 to 10 minutes DM	6 to 10 minutes DM
Sweet potato, whole	50 to 60 minutes IM	50 to 60 minutes DL
Sweet potato, 5mm slices	8 to 10 minutes DM	8 to 10 minutes DM

Vegetables	Grilling Time for Gas/Charcoal	Grilling Time for Weber® Q™ and Baby Q™
Tomato: garden, 1cm slices	2 to 4 minutes DM	2 to 4 minutes DM
Tomato: garden, halved	6 to 8 minutes DM	6 to 8 minutes DM
Tomato: plum, halved	6 to 8 minutes DM	6 to 8 minutes DM
Tomato: plum, whole	8 to 10 minutes DM	8 to 10 minutes DM

Fruit	Grilling Time for Gas/Charcoal	Grilling Time for Weber® Q™ and Baby Q™
Apple, whole	35 to 40 minutes IM	
Apple, 1cm thick slices	4 to 6 minutes DM	4 to 6 minutes DM
Apricot, halved, pit removed	6 to 8 minutes DM	6 to 8 minutes DM
Banana, halved lengthways	6 to 8 minutes DM	6 to 8 minutes DM
Nectarine, halved lengthways, pit removed	8 to 10 minutes DM	8 to 10 minutes DM
Peach, halved lengthways, pit removed	8 to 10 minutes DM	8 to 10 minutes DM
Pear, halved lengthways	10 to 12 minutes DM	10 to 12 minutes DM
Pineapple, peeled and cored, 1cm slices or 2.5cm wedges	5 to 10 minutes DM	5 to 10 minutes DM
Strawberry	4 to 5 minutes DM	4 to 5 minutes DM

Note: Grilling times for fruit will depend on ripeness.

GARLIC

This ingredient is widely used to add flavour to even the most simple of dishes. Peel and crush a bulb and add it to a marinade for meat, poultry or fish.

GINGER

Ginger is a versatile spice and can be used in a variety of sweet and savoury recipes. It originates from Southeast Asia. If bought fresh and firm it will keep for a week or so.

Flavours

CINNAMON

A spice most of us are familiar with, cinnamon is used in a variety of cuisines, most notably middle eastern, Mexican and North African. Cinnamon is actually stripped bark from either evergreen or cassia trees and is available in whole sticks or ground.

LEMON

Lemon wedges are a common accompaniment to fish dishes and are often used to add a citrus flavour to a wide variety of recipes. Lemon halves barbecued on the grill will cook to a lovely gooey caramelized consistency and really add a twist to any basic barbecue recipe.

HONEY

Honey is the natural nectar of a flower converted to a golden syrup by bees. The flavour of honey depends on what the bees have been feeding on and can range from lavender and eucalyptus to clover and heather varieties.

CHILLI

There are more than 1000 varieties of chilli all with varying degrees of heat. This hot flavour can be used to add a kick to any recipe. You can add as much or as little as your taste buds can stand!

MUSTARD

Pungent and flavourful, mustard has remained an important condiment throughout the ages. It is available in whole seeds, as a powder, or "flour," and, most popular, as a prepared paste. The sharp flavour complements meat, poultry and fish, just to name a few.

CHAPTER ONE
Appetizers

Potato Wedges
with Soured Cream & Coriander Dip

Gas Direct Medium Heat / **Weber® Q™** Direct Medium Heat / **Charcoal** Direct
Prep time 15 minutes + chilling time for dip / **Grilling time** 10 to 15 minutes / **Serves** 4

For the dip:
100g cream cheese
150ml soured cream
1 tablespoon fresh chopped
coriander, or to taste
1 garlic clove, crushed
(or to taste)
Salt and freshly ground
black pepper, divided

For the wedges:
900g potatoes, unpeeled,
scrubbed and drained
3 tablespoons olive oil
½ teaspoon paprika, or
to taste

1. Beat together all the ingredients for the dip. Cover and chill until required (for up to 4 hours).

2. Cut the potatoes first in half and then into even-sized wedges. Stir together the olive oil and paprika, season with salt and pepper and then toss the potato wedges in this mix.

3. Using tongs, carefully arrange the potato wedges on the grill and barbecue over Direct Medium heat for 10 to 15 minutes or until golden brown, crisp and cooked all the way through, turning once. Transfer the wedges to a large platter. Serve hot with the soured cream and coriander dip.

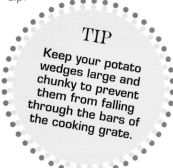

TIP
Keep your potato wedges large and chunky to prevent them from falling through the bars of the cooking grate.

Gooey Camembert
with Herby Toasted Strips

Gas Direct Medium Heat / **Weber® Q™** Direct Medium Heat / **Charcoal** Direct
Prep time 15 minutes / **Grilling time** 10 minutes / **Serves** 4

250g whole Camembert in a wooden box
1 tablespoon vodka

For the toasted strips:
8 tablespoons basil-flavoured olive oil
Sea salt and freshly ground black pepper
2 tablespoon fresh chopped mint or parsley
6 slices white bread, crusts removed and cut into 24 strips

1. Unwrap the Camembert, remove any packaging and put the cheese back in the bottom half of its wooden box. Place the box in a foil container which is suitable for cooking on a barbecue (the Weber small drip pan is ideal), pierce the rind several times with a skewer and slowly drizzle over the vodka.

2. Barbecue over Direct Medium heat for 6 to 8 minutes until the cheese is just runny under the rind (the exact cooking time depends on how ripe the cheese is). Remove from the grill using oven gloves. Leave to stand for 1 minute, then carefully turn out onto a plate and remove the box.

3. Mix together the basil-flavoured olive oil, seasoning and mint, and brush both sides of the bread strips with this herby oil mix. Pop on the barbecue and cook over Direct Medium heat until golden (this only takes about 1 minute each side).

4. Carefully lift up the rind to reveal the lovely gooey Camembert and serve with the herby toast.

Garlic Herby Bread
with Houmous

Gas Direct Medium Heat / **Weber® Q™** Direct Medium Heat / **Charcoal** Direct
Prep time 15 minutes + plus chilling / **Grilling time** 2 to 4 minutes / **Serves** 4

For the dip:
**410g can chickpeas, rinsed
   and drained**
**Juice of 1½ lemons (or
   to taste)**
**1 to 2 garlic cloves,
   crushed**
2 to 3 tablespoons tahini
**5 tablespoons olive oil, plus
   a little extra**
1 tablespoon sesame oil
**Salt and freshly ground
   black pepper, divided**

For the bread:
**6 tablespoons garlic-
   flavoured olive oil**
**2 fresh rosemary sprigs,
   leaves separated and
   chopped**
1 loaf ciabatta bread, sliced

1. Tip the chickpeas into a blender or food processor with 2 to 4 tablespoons of cold water. Add the lemon juice and garlic, and whiz to a thick purée. Add the tahini and whiz again. Keeping the motor running, gradually add the 5 tablespoons of olive oil and the sesame oil. Season to taste with salt, pepper and more lemon juice if necessary. Spoon into a bowl, drizzle with a little extra olive oil, cover and chill for up to 2 hours.

2. Mix together the garlic-flavoured olive oil, rosemary and seasoning. Lightly brush the slices of bread with the herb oil and barbecue over Direct Medium heat for 1 to 2 minutes on each side or until golden on both sides. Serve the hot crispy garlic bread with the houmous.

Lip-smacking Ribs

Gas Indirect Medium Heat / **Weber® Q™** Direct Low Heat / **Charcoal** Indirect
Prep time 15 minutes + 15 minutes marinating / **Grilling time** 15 to 20 minutes / **Serves** 4

1.5kg pork spare ribs

For the marinade:
**4 tablespoons dark soy
  sauce**
**4 tablespoons light brown
  sugar**
**2 tablespoons black bean
  sauce**
**1 teaspoon sweet chilli
  sauce**
150ml fresh orange juice
**Salt and freshly ground
  black pepper**

1. Mix together all the ingredients for the marinade and simmer in a small pan for a few minutes, then pour over the pork. Carefully turn over the ribs so they are well coated in the marinade. Leave them to stand for 15 minutes, turning them once or twice.

2. Lift out the ribs and discard the marinade. Barbecue them over Indirect Medium heat (or Direct Low on the Weber® Q™ gas grills) for 15 to 20 minutes, turning after 10 minutes, or until tender and cooked all the way through. Leave to stand for 5 to 10 minutes covered with foil before serving.

TIP
For a speedy clean up, marinate your barbecue meats in a plastic food bag.

Seared Scallops
with Summer Leaves

Gas Direct High Heat / **Weber® Q™** Direct High Heat / **Charcoal** Direct
Prep time 10 minutes / **Grilling time** 4 to 5 minutes / **Serves** 4

**12 large fresh scallops,
  trimmed**
**35g butter, melted and
  cooled**
**2 tablespoons olive oil, plus
  a little extra (optional)**
Juice of 1 lime
**Salt and freshly ground
  black pepper**
50g mixed leaf salad

1. Put the scallops in a large bowl and add the butter, 1 tablespoon of olive oil, lime juice and seasoning. Stir together gently.

2. Remove the scallops and discard any leftover butter mix. Carefully arrange them on the grill, making sure they don't fall through, and barbecue over Direct High heat for 4 to 5 minutes, turning once, until just tender and cooked.

3. Divide the salad between four plates, drizzle over a little extra oil, if desired, and serve the scallops on top.

TIP

Keep a close eye on the scallops while they are being grilled as they are very easy to overcook.

Ciabatta Pizzas
with Hot Tomatoes, Mozzarella & Wild Rocket

Gas Direct Medium Heat / **Weber® Q™** Direct Medium Heat / **Charcoal** Direct
Prep time 10 minutes / **Grilling time** 7 to 8 minutes / **Serves** 4

**3 tablespoons olive oil, plus
    a little extra (optional)**
2 garlic cloves, crushed
**Sea salt and freshly ground
    black pepper**
4 midi plum tomatoes
4 slices ciabatta bread
**150g mozzarella cheese
    (drained weight) sliced
    into four**
**10g wild rocket, washed
    and drained**

1. Mix together the 3 tablespoons of olive oil, garlic and seasoning. Cut the tomatoes in half, brush with a little garlic oil and arrange in a foil container suitable for cooking on the barbecue (the Weber drip pan is ideal). Barbecue cut-side up over Direct Medium heat for about 3 minutes, or until the tomatoes start to char. Remove from the grill.

2. Brush one side of the ciabatta with the remaining oil and cook over Direct Medium heat for 2 minutes, turning once, or until toasted on both sides. Remove the small drip pan from the barbecue with tongs or oven gloves.

3. Pop the toasted bread in the foil container or drip pan, put a slice of mozzarella on top followed by two tomato halves and continue cooking for a further 2 to 3 minutes, or until the cheese is melted. Remove the ciabatta pizzas from the grill, garnish with wild rocket and serve with a twist of black pepper and a drizzle of olive oil, if desired.

TIP

If cooking on charcoal, try adding basil stalks to the coals for added flavour.

CHAPTER TWO

Fish & Shellfish

Skewered Monkfish
with Green Rice

Gas Direct Medium Heat / **Weber® Q™** Direct Medium Heat / **Charcoal** Direct
Prep time 25 minutes / **Grilling time** 8 to 10 minutes / **Serves** 4

For the kebabs:

500g skinless, boneless
   monkfish fillet
12 rashers rindless streaky
   bacon, weighing about
   150g
1 lime, cut into eighths
16 fresh bay leaves
3 tablespoons olive oil

For the rice:

200g basmati rice, washed
Salt and freshly ground
   black pepper
2 tablespoons green
   tapenade or pesto
2 tablespoons fresh
   chopped tarragon

1. Cut the monkfish into cubes. Stretch the bacon with the back of a knife and cut in half. Onto eight metal skewers thread the lime, monkfish, bacon (concertinered) and bay leaf alternately until it has all been used.

2. Brush with olive oil and barbecue over Direct Medium heat for 8 to 10 minutes, turning once.

3. Meanwhile, cook the rice according to the packet instructions (about 10 minutes). Drain and season with salt, freshly ground black pepper, green tapenade or pesto and fresh herbs.

4. Serve the skewered monkfish with the green rice.

Succulent Seared Tuna

Gas Direct Medium Heat / **Weber® Q™** Direct Medium Heat / **Charcoal** Direct
Prep time 15 minutes + 30 minutes marinating / **Grilling time** 8 to 10 minutes / **Serves** 4

**4 tuna steaks, each
  weighing about 200g**
Lime wedges, to garnish

For the marinade:
**4cm piece fresh root ginger,
  peeled and grated**
**1 mild red chilli, deseeded
  and finely chopped**
**Grated rind and juice of
  2 limes**
¼ teaspoon salt
3 tablespoons sesame oil
1 tablespoon oyster sauce

1. Place the tuna steaks in a large non-metallic dish. Mix together the ingredients for the marinade and pour it over. Turn the steaks, cover with clingfilm and leave to marinate in the refrigerator for 30 minutes.

2. Remove the steaks and discard the marinade. Barbecue over Direct Medium heat for 8 to 10 minutes (the exact cooking time depends on the thickness of the fish), turning once, or until the fish is cooked through. Serve garnished with lime wedges, green rice (see page 44) and a little mixed salad if desired.

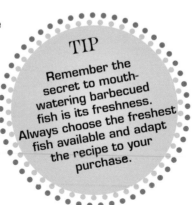

TIP
Remember the secret to mouth-watering barbecued fish is its freshness. Always choose the freshest fish available and adapt the recipe to your purchase.

Greek-style Roast Sea Bass

Gas Indirect Medium Heat / **Weber® Q™** Direct Medium Heat / **Charcoal** Indirect
Prep time 15 minutes / **Grilling time** 10 to 20 minutes / **Serves** 2

**2 whole sea bass, each
weighing about 350g
scaled, gutted and fins
trimmed**
**Salt and freshly ground
black pepper**
4 tablespoons olive oil
**2 tablespoons chopped
black olives**
**1 preserved lemon, drained
and chopped**
**2 bunches fresh thyme,
weighing about 10g total**

1. Wash the fish inside and out and pat dry with kitchen paper. Make three slashes in both sides of the fish and season inside and out with salt and freshly ground black pepper. Mix together 2 tablespoons of olive oil, the chopped olives and lemon. Use this mixture to fill the cavity of the fish, followed by most of the thyme.

2. Brush the outside of the sea bass with the remaining oil and barbecue over Indirect Medium heat for 15 to 20 minutes (or over Direct Medium heat for 10 to 15 minutes on the Weber® Q™ gas grills), turning once halfway through. Serve garnished with the reserved thyme.

TIP
To check fish is cooked through to the centre, insert the tip of a knife into the thickest part of the fish then remove and carefully check if the tip is hot.

Halibut
with Lime & Tarragon Butter

Gas Direct Medium Heat / **Weber® Q™** Direct Medium Heat / **Charcoal** Direct
Prep time 15 minutes / **Grilling time** 10 to 12 minutes / **Serves** 4

**4 halibut steaks, each
  weighing about 175g
Salt and freshly ground
  black pepper
100g butter
Grated rind and juice of
  1 lime
2 tablespoons fresh
  chopped tarragon**

1. Season the halibut with salt and freshly ground black pepper.

2. For the seasoned butter, blend together the remaining ingredients in a food processor.

3. Set half the butter aside. Melt the rest in a small pan and brush over both sides of the fish, discarding any that is left.

4. Barbecue the fish over Direct Medium heat for 10 to 12 minutes, or until tender, turning once halfway through cooking (the exact cooking time depends on the thickness of the fish). Serve dotted with the reserved butter and couscous if desired.

TIP
Don't leave raw food sitting out in the sun before cooking. Keep it well covered – and cool – inside.

Skewered Prosciutto-wrapped Scallops

Gas Direct High Heat / **Weber® Q™** Direct High Heat / **Charcoal** Direct
Prep time 15 minutes / **Grilling time** 4 to 6 minutes / **Serves** 4

**16 large fresh scallops,
trimmed**
**16 strips of prosciutto, cut
the same width as the
scallops (usually 8 slices,
halved)**
1 tablespoon olive oil
Juice of 1 lime
Freshly ground black pepper

1. Put the scallops on a board and wrap each of them in a strip of prosciutto.

2. Mix together the olive oil, lime juice and black pepper.

3. Dip the scallops in the oil mixture one at a time and thread onto four metal skewers, discarding any leftover lime mixture. Barbecue over Direct High heat for 4 to 6 minutes, carefully turning once, until just tender.

TIP

Scallops are available both fresh and frozen. Fresh scallops should have a sweet smell and can vary between light beige and pale pink in colour.

Moroccan Spiced Swordfish

Gas Direct Medium Heat / **Weber® Q™** Direct Medium Heat / **Charcoal** Direct
Prep time 15 minutes + 30 minutes marinating / **Grilling time** 10 to 12 minutes / **Serves** 2

**2 swordfish steaks, each
   weighing about 200g
Oil, for brushing**

For the marinade:
**A handful of fresh coriander
2 garlic cloves
1 teaspoon paprika
1 teaspoon ground cumin
1 teaspoon ground
   coriander
2 tablespoons lemon juice
2 tablespoons olive oil**

1. In a food processor whiz together all the ingredients for the marinade. Brush the swordfish steaks on both sides with this spiced herb mixture, place in a non-metallic dish, cover and chill for 30 minutes.

2. Remove the steaks and discard the marinade. Brush the fish with a little oil to prevent sticking. Barbecue over Direct Medium heat for 10 to 12 minutes, turning once, until cooked through.

TIP
Thoroughly wash your hands, utensils, chopping boards and work surfaces after preparing raw fish and shellfish. Squeeze fresh juice over your surface to freshen.

Crab Cakes
with Dill Dip

Gas Direct High Heat / **Weber® Q™** Direct High Heat / **Charcoal** Direct
Prep time 15 minutes + 1 hour chilling / **Grilling time** 6 to 10 minutes / **Serves** 4

For the crab cakes:
**400g cold cooked, lightly
   mashed potato (made
   without milk or butter)**
1 tablespoon egg white
Anchovy sauce to taste
4 x 43g tins dressed crab
**Salt and freshly ground
   black pepper**
Oil, for brushing
**Lime wedges and finely
   chopped red and green
   pepper, to garnish**

For the dip:
**150ml full-fat natural
   yogurt**
**3 tablespoons freshly
   chopped dill**

1. Put the lightly mashed potato into a bowl and beat in the egg white, anchovy sauce, dressed crab, salt and pepper. Cover and chill for about 1 hour to allow the mixture to firm up.

2. Put the crab cake mixture on a board, divide into four portions and shape each portion into three small cake shapes using floured hands. Brush on both sides with oil and barbecue over Direct High heat for 6 to 8 minutes (or 8 to 10 minutes on the Weber® Q™ gas grills), turning carefully once halfway through using a fish slice.

3. Mix together the dip ingredients and serve with the hot crab cakes and garnish with lime wedges and chopped red and green peppers.

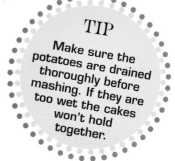

TIP

Make sure the potatoes are drained thoroughly before mashing. If they are too wet the cakes won't hold together.

Sticky Prawns on Skewers

Gas Direct Medium Heat / **Weber® Q™** Direct Medium Heat / **Charcoal** Direct
Prep time 15 minutes / **Grilling time** 4 to 7 minutes / **Serves** 4

12 wooden skewers
36 raw king prawns,
   heads removed, shelled
   and deveined
Juice of 2 limes

For the marinade:
3 tablespoons clear honey
5 tablespoons dark soy
   sauce
1 tablespoon chilli sauce
2 tablespoons olive oil

1. Place 12 wooden skewers in cold water and leave them to soak for 30 minutes.

2. Place the prawns into a non-metallic dish and drizzle over the lime juice. Stir well, so they are evenly coated, and leave for 5 minutes to allow the flavour to infuse.

3. Mix together the honey, soy sauce, chilli sauce and olive oil, and pour over the prawns. Stir the mixture well so the prawns are nicely coated in the marinade.

4. Remove the prawns and discard the marinade. Remove the skewers from the water and pat dry. Thread the prawns onto the skewers, leaving space between them and brush with oil.

5. Barbecue the skewers over Direct Medium heat for 4 to 7 minutes until the prawns turn pink (the exact time depends on the size of the prawns), turning once halfway through, until they are cooked through.

Salmon Teriyaki

Gas Direct Medium Heat / **Weber® Q™** Direct Medium Heat / **Charcoal** Direct
Prep time 15 minutes + 1 hour marinating / **Grilling time** 8 to 10 minutes / **Serves** 4

**4 salmon steaks, each
  weighing about 200g**
Oil, for brushing
**2 spring onions, trimmed
  and cut into fine strips,
  and fresh coriander
  leaves, to garnish**

For the marinade:
100ml soy sauce
100ml dry sherry
**100ml sake or rice wine
  vinegar**
**2 tablespoons soft brown
  sugar**
**¼ teaspoon of crushed
  chilli flakes, according
  to taste**

1. Arrange the salmon steaks in a single layer in a non-metallic dish. Mix together the ingredients for the marinade and pour it over. Turn the steaks, cover and chill for about 1 hour.

2. Drain the salmon and discard the marinade. Brush the steaks with oil, then barbecue them over Direct Medium heat for about 8 to 10 minutes, turning once halfway through cooking.

3. Serve garnished with strips of spring onion and a scattering of fresh coriander leaves.

TIP

Do as much of the preparation – all that chopping and marinating – in advance so the actual cooking is quick, easy and enjoyable.

CHAPTER THREE

Poultry

Five-spice Roast Chicken

Gas Indirect Medium Heat / **Weber® Q™** Direct Low Heat / **Charcoal** Indirect
Prep time 15 minutes / **Grilling time** 1¼ to 1½ hours / **Serves** 4

- **1 tablespoon Chinese five-spice powder**
- **1.5kg free-range chicken**
- **1 lemon, halved and cut into wedges**
- **1 small bunch fresh coriander, tied with string**
- **50g butter**
- **2 tablespoons dark soy sauce**
- **2 tablespoons dry sherry**

1. Liberally season the cavity and the outside of the chicken with Chinese five-spice powder. Then fill the cavity with the lemon wedges and coriander. Tie the chicken securely with string so that it stays in a good shape during cooking.

2. Heat together the butter, soy sauce and sherry and simmer until reduced. Brush this mixture over the chicken, discarding any that is left over. Put the chicken in a roasting rack and place this on the grill. Barbecue over Indirect Medium heat (or Direct Low heat on the Weber® Q™ gas grills) for 1¼ to 1½ hours, or until the juices run clear.

3. Carefully remove the chicken from the grill, cover with foil and leave to stand for 10 to 15 minutes before carving and serving.

TIP

If you decide to add stuffing to your roast chicken, cook it in a foil tray on top of the cooking grate while the bird is barbecuing.

Coconut Chicken Skewers
with Red Rice

Gas Direct Medium Heat / **Weber® Q™** Direct Medium Heat / **Charcoal** Direct
Prep time 20 minutes + 25 minutes marinating / **Grilling time** 8 to 10 minutes / **Serves** 4

12 wooden skewers
4 skinless, boneless chicken
breasts, each weighing
about 175g, cut into
2.5cm cubes
Oil, for brushing

For the marinade:
250ml coconut milk
1 mild red chilli, deseeded
and sliced
Grated zest and juice of
1 lime
1 garlic clove, crushed
3cm piece root ginger,
peeled and grated

For the rice:
250g red rice
2 tablespoons fresh
chopped coriander
Salt and freshly ground
black pepper

1. Place 12 wooden skewers in cold water and leave them to soak for 30 minutes.

2. Stir together the ingredients for the marinade and tip into a shallow dish. Add the chicken cubes, mix well, cover and chill for 25 minutes.

3. Remove the chicken and discard the marinade. Remove the skewers from the water and pat dry. Divide into twelve piles and thread the cubes onto the skewers.

4. Brush with oil and barbecue over Direct Medium heat for 8 to 10 minutes, or until the chicken is cooked through, turning once.

5. Meanwhile, cook the rice according to the packet instructions, drain, stir in the coriander and season. Put a portion of rice on each plate and three skewers on top.

Crispy Orange Chicken Legs

Gas Indirect Medium Heat / **Weber® Q™** Direct Low Heat / **Charcoal** Indirect
Prep time 10 minutes + 1 hour marinating / **Grilling time** 40 to 50 minutes / **Serves** 4

**4 whole chicken legs, each
weighing about 250g**
**1 tablespoon thick-cut
orange marmalade,
melted**
50g butter, melted
1 tablespoon hoisin sauce
**4 tablespoons freshly
squeezed orange juice**
Oil, for brushing

1. Cut off any excess fat, then make deep slashes in the chicken legs and arrange them in a single layer in a non-metallic dish. Mix together the marmalade, butter, hoisin sauce and orange juice, and brush over both sides of the chicken legs. Discard any leftover marinade. Cover and leave to marinate in the refrigerator for 1 hour.

2. Remove the chicken and discard the marinade. Brush with oil and barbecue the legs, boneside down, over Indirect Medium heat for 20 minutes (or Direct Low heat for 15 to 20 minutes on the Weber® Q™ gas grills), then turn and cook for a further 20 to 25 minutes (or a further 15 to 20 minutes on the Weber® Q™ gas grills), or until the chicken is tender and the juices run clear.

3. Remove from the grill, cover with foil and leave to rest for 5 minutes before serving.

Cheese-stuffed Chicken Fillets
wrapped in Pancetta

Gas Direct Medium Heat / **Weber® Q™** Direct Medium Heat / **Charcoal** Direct
Prep time 15 minutes / **Grilling time** 12 to 16 minutes / **Serves** 4

4 wooden skewers
4 skinless, boneless chicken breasts, each weighing about 150 to 175g
4 chunky slices of Cheddar cheese, each weighing about 15g
1 tablespoon snipped fresh chives
Freshly ground black pepper
8 slices of smoked pancetta, or about 70g
Oil, for brushing

1. Place 4 wooden skewers in cold water and leave them to soak for 30 minutes.

2. Using a very sharp knife, carefully make a horizontal slit from the side in each chicken breast so the cheese will fit in neatly. Push the Cheddar into the slit, then sprinkle with chives and black pepper.

3. Remove the skewers from the water and pat dry. Wrap each breast in two slices of pancetta and pierce with a skewer to hold in place.

4. Brush with oil and barbecue over Direct Medium heat for 12 to 16 minutes, turning once, or until the breasts are cooked through. Remove from the grill, cover with foil and leave to stand for 5 minutes.

TIP
Always keep raw and cooked food completely separate (to avoid cross-contamination).

Char-grilled Chicken Breasts
with Harissa

Gas Direct Medium Heat / **Weber® Q™** Direct Medium Heat / **Charcoal** Direct
Prep time 10 minutes + 1 hour marinating / **Grilling time** 10 to 12 minutes / **Serves** 4

1 ciabatta loaf
4 boneless, skinless chicken breasts, each weighing about 175g
1 tablespoon fresh chopped coriander
25g wild rocket, washed and drained, to serve
Lime wedges and red onion slices, to garnish

For the marinade:
Grated rind and juice of 2 limes, divided
2 teaspoons harissa
8 tablespoons olive oil, divided

1. Cut the ciabatta loaf in half horizontally and then cut each half into 4 chunks to make 8 pieces in total.

2. Cut slits in the chicken breasts to allow the marinade flavours to penetrate and arrange in a single layer in a non-metallic dish.

3. To make the marinade, mix together the grated rind and juice of 1 lime, the harissa paste and 2 tablespoons of olive oil. Brush over both sides of the chicken, cover and leave in the refrigerator to marinate for 1 hour.

4. Drain the chicken breasts and discard the marinade. Barbecue over Direct Medium heat for 10 to 12 minutes, turning once, or until the breasts are cooked through.

5. Brush the ciabatta chunks with oil and barbecue over Direct Medium heat for 2 minutes on each side.

6. Arrange the chicken on the ciabatta. Mix together the remaining lime juice and olive oil with the coriander, and drizzle over the meat. Top the chicken with the remaining ciabatta pieces and serve immediately with fresh rocket.

Turkey Escalopes
with Bang Bang Dressing

Gas Direct Medium Heat / **Weber® Q™** Direct Medium Heat / **Charcoal** Direct
Prep time 20 minutes / **Grilling time** 5 to 7 minutes / **Serves** 4

**4 turkey escalopes about
  5mm to 1cm thick**
Oil, for brushing
Fresh green salad, to serve

For the bang bang dressing:
2 tablespoons sesame oil
**1 small onion, finely
  chopped**
**1 mild red chilli, deseeded
  and finely chopped**
1 garlic clove, crushed
**2.5cm piece fresh root
  ginger, peeled and finely
  chopped**
75g salted peanuts
300ml chicken stock

1. To make the dressing, heat the sesame oil in a pan, add the onion, chilli, garlic and ginger, and cook for about 5 minutes, or until softened but not coloured. Add the peanuts, stir gently and heat for about 3 minutes. Add the stock, bring to the boil then simmer for 2 to 3 minutes.

2. Remove from the heat and whiz in a food processor or liquidizer until thickened and smooth. Leave to cool.

3. Brush the turkey escalopes with the olive oil and barbecue over Direct Medium heat for 3 to 4 minutes. Turn over and cook for a further 2 to 3 minutes, or until tender and cooked through.

4. Remove the escalopes to a board and slice. Arrange the slices on a plate, add a little salad on top and serve with a bowl of the bang bang dressing.

Turkey with Chermoula

Gas Direct Medium Heat / **Weber® Q™** Direct Medium Heat / **Charcoal** Direct
Prep time 10 minutes + 20 minutes marinating / **Grilling time** 8 to 10 minutes / **Serves** 4

**4 turkey breast steaks,
  each weighing about 125g**

For the chermoula:

**15g fresh flat-leaf parsley,
  trimmed of stalks**
**15g fresh coriander,
  trimmed of stalks**
6 tablespoons olive oil
Juice of 1 lemon
2 large garlic cloves
1 teaspoon paprika
1 teaspoon ground cumin
¼ teaspoon salt

1. Place the turkey breast steaks in a large dish. Whiz together the chermoula ingredients in a food processor to make a paste and spread this over both sides of the turkey. Turn so it is coated in the mix. Cover with clingfilm and leave to marinate in the refrigerator for 20 minutes to allow the flavours to penetrate the meat.

2. Barbecue the turkey over Direct Medium heat for 8 to 10 minutes, turning once halfway through, or until the turkey is cooked (the exact cooking time will depend on the thickness of the meat). Cover with foil and leave to rest for 5 minutes before serving.

TIP

Other flavours that work well with turkey or chicken are tarragon, basil, thyme, rosemary, ginger, chilli, saffron and sherry.

Tikka-style Turkey Kebabs

Gas Direct Medium Heat / **Weber® Q™** Direct Medium Heat / **Charcoal** Direct
Prep time 15 minutes + 30 minutes marinating / **Grilling time** 8 to 12 minutes / **Serves** 6

550g skinless turkey breast fillet, cut into 2.5cm cubes
2 red peppers, halved, deseeded and cut into chunks
420g jar spicy tikka masala cooking sauce
Oil, for brushing

1. Put the turkey cubes and pepper chunks into a medium-sized dish. Pour over the cooking sauce and mix well. Cover with clingfilm and chill for 30 minutes to allow the flavours to develop.

2. Thread the turkey cubes and pepper chunks alternately onto 6 metal skewers and discard any leftover sauce. Brush the skewers with oil and barbecue over Direct Medium heat for 8 to 12 minutes, or until the turkey is cooked through, turning once halfway through cooking.

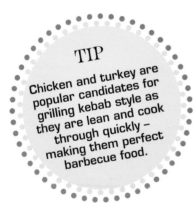

TIP

Chicken and turkey are popular candidates for grilling kebab style as they are lean and cook through quickly – making them perfect barbecue food.

Chinese-style Duck

Gas Direct Low Heat / **Weber® Q™** Direct Low Heat / **Charcoal** Direct
Prep time 15 minutes + 2 hours marinating / **Grilling time** 14 to 15 minutes / **Serves** 4

**4 boneless duck breasts
each weighing about
250–300g and about
1.5cm thick**

For the marinade:
**2 tablespoons dark soy
sauce
4 tablespoons hoisin sauce
1 tablespoon Chinese hot
chilli sauce
2 garlic cloves, crushed
2.5cm piece fresh root
ginger, peeled and grated**

1. Using a sharp knife, trim the skin from the duck breasts to 3mm and cut off any excess fat that overhangs the edge of the meat. Score the remaining fat into a diamond pattern, cutting right through to the flesh (this helps the excess fat drain away). Arrange in a single layer in a non-metallic dish.

2. Mix together the ingredients for the marinade, then pour it over the duck breasts and turn them so they are well coated. Cover and chill for about 2 hours.

3. Drain the duck breasts and discard the marinade. Barbecue over Direct Low heat for 7 to 8 minutes, or until the skin is golden. Turn and cook for a further 6 to 7 minutes, or until they are just firm to touch, for medium-cooked duck or for a further 3 to 4 minutes for well done.

4. Cover with foil and leave to stand for 5 minutes before serving.

Herb Buttered Spatchcock Poussins

Gas Indirect Medium Heat / **Weber® Q™** Direct Low Heat / **Charcoal** Indirect
Prep time 15 minutes / **Grilling time** 40 to 50 minutes / **Serves** 2

4 wooden skewers
2 poussins, spatchcocked
50g butter
2 garlic cloves, crushed
3 tablespoons fresh
 chopped herbs such as
 tarragon, marjoram
 and parsley
Salt and freshly ground
 black pepper
Tomato and herb salad,
 to serve

1. Place 4 wooden skewers in cold water and leave them to soak for 30 minutes. Remove them from the water and pat dry before use.

2. Using two skewers per poussin, pierce the bird diagonally (in at the wing on one side and out at the leg on the other) with one, then repeat in the opposite direction with the other.

3. Melt together the butter, garlic, herbs and seasoning, and brush on both sides of the poussins. Discard any leftover melted butter.

4. Barbecue the poussins boneside down over Indirect Medium heat (or over Direct Low on the Weber® Q™ gas grills) for 25 minutes, then turn and cook for a further 15 to 25 minutes. Check the juices run clear from the thickest part of the thigh before removing them from the grill.

5. Serve with a fresh tomato and herb salad.

TIP

A spatchcocked bird lets you barbecue flat on the grate and cuts down your cooking time.

CHAPTER FOUR

Meat

Succulent Steaks
with Boursin Butter

Gas Direct High Heat / **Weber® Q™** Direct High Heat / **Charcoal** Direct / **Prep time** 15 minutes + chilling butter / **Grilling time** 2cm thick 6 to 8 minutes; 2.5cm thick 8 to 10 minutes / **Serves** 4

50g butter, softened
30g Boursin flavoured with garlic and herbs
1 tablespoon fresh chopped parsley
Salt and freshly ground black pepper
4 prime fillet beef steaks, each weighing about 200g
1 to 2 tablespoons olive oil
250g bundle asparagus, trimmed, blanched and drained
16 cherry tomatoes on the vine
Salt and freshly ground black pepper

1. Beat together the butter, Boursin, parsley and seasoning, and roll into a log using clingfilm. Chill until hard enough to cut into four slices.

2. Season the fillet steaks, brush lightly with olive oil and barbecue over Direct High heat for 3 to 5 minutes each side, turning once.

3. Remove the steaks from the grill, add a slice of Boursin butter, cover with foil and then leave to rest for 5 minutes. This allows the juices to settle (for a fuller flavour) and the butter to melt over the meat.

4. Toss the asparagus tips and cherry tomatoes in olive oil and place on the barbecue for a couple of minutes on each side. Season to taste and serve with the steaks.

Flash Grill Peppered Beef Wraps

Gas Direct Medium Heat / **Weber® Q™** Direct Medium Heat / **Charcoal** Direct
Prep time 10 minutes / **Grilling time** 10 to 15 minutes / **Makes** 4

**650g piece rump steak cut
  2.5cm thick and trimmed
  of excess fat**
**1 tablespoon freshly
  crushed black pepper**
A little light olive oil
**4 soft flour tortillas,
  to serve**
**4 tablespoons guacamole,
  to serve**
**4 tablespoons tomato salsa,
  to serve**
**4 tablespoons soured
  cream, to serve**
**A handful of little gem
  lettuce leaves, to serve**

1. Put the steak on a sheet of clingfilm and scatter over the black pepper. Turn the steak, shaking off any excess, and press on the other side.

2. Brush the steaks with a little olive oil and barbecue over Direct Medium heat for 10 to 15 minutes, turning once. Remove from the grill, cover with foil and leave to rest for 5 to 10 minutes before slicing on the diagonal across the grain.

3. Barbecue the tortillas for a few seconds on each side, just to let them warm through – don't cook them so long they become crisp or difficult to roll up! Place the steak slices on the warm tortillas, spread over a dollop of guacamole, tomato salsa, soured cream and a little lettuce. Roll up and serve.

Hot Beef Sandwich
with Horseradish Sauce

Gas Direct Medium Heat / **Weber® Q™** Direct Medium Heat / **Charcoal** Direct
Prep time 5 minutes / **Grilling time** 10 to 15 minutes / **Makes** 4

**2 sirloin steaks, each
weighing about 325g, cut
3cm thick, trimmed of
excess fat**
1 tablespoon sunflower oil
**Salt and freshly ground
black pepper**
8 slices of bread, to serve
**2 to 4 tablespoons creamed
horseradish sauce,
to serve**
**Mixed green salad, washed
and drained, to serve**

1. Put the steaks in a non-metallic dish. Brush on both sides with sunflower oil and season.

2. Barbecue the steaks over Direct Medium heat for 10 to 15 minutes, turning once halfway through cooking. Remove the steak from the grill, cover with foil and leave to rest for 5 to 10 minutes.

3. Slice the meat thinly across the grain. Butter the bread if desired, then spread with horseradish to taste, add the salad and arrange the beef slices on top. Top with another slice of bread and serve.

TIP
Use tongs for turning meats; a fork will pierce the meat and allow the juices to escape.

Spicy Rub Steaks

Gas Direct Medium Heat / **Weber® Q™** Direct Medium Heat / **Charcoal** Direct
Prep time 15 minutes / **Grilling time** 8 to 12 minutes / **Serves** 2

2 sirloin steaks, each weighing about 225g and about 2.5cm thick

For the rub:
1 teaspoon medium chilli powder
1 teaspoon paprika
1 teaspoon dry mustard
1 teaspoon ground coriander
2 garlic cloves, crushed
1 teaspoon salt
4 tablespoons light olive oil

1. Trim any excess fat from the steaks.

2. Put all the ingredients for the rub in a food processor and whiz together. Brush onto both sides of the steaks and rub in well.

3. Barbecue the steaks over Direct Medium heat for 8 to 12 minutes, turning once. Remove from the grill and leave to rest covered in foil for 5 to 10 minutes before serving.

TIP

Try varying the flavours and spices in the rub according to your personal taste. Other flavours that work well with beef include cinnamon, ginger, cardamom, peppercorns, brandy, port, horseradish, mustard and soy sauce.

Pork Steaks
with Caramelized Apple

Gas Direct Medium Heat / **Weber® Q™** Direct Medium Heat / **Charcoal** Direct
Prep time 15 minutes / **Grilling time** 18 to 22 minutes / **Serves** 4

**4 pork loin steaks, about
2.5cm, trimmed of fat,
each weighing about 175g
Salt and freshly ground
black pepper
2 tablespoons toasted
sesame oil
Juice of 1 lime
2 teaspoons honey
1 teaspoon Dijon mustard,
or to taste
4 eating apples, cored and
cut into eighths
1 tablespoon clear honey
1 tablespoon oil**

1. Season both sides of the pork steaks with salt and pepper. Mix together the sesame oil, lime juice, honey and Dijon mustard and brush onto the meat.

2. Barbecue the steaks over Direct Medium heat for 10 to 14 minutes, turning once halfway through cooking (the exact cooking time depends on the thickness of the meat). Remove the steaks from the grill and leave to stand for 5 to 10 minutes covered in foil.

3. Meanwhile, toss the apple pieces in the honey and oil and barbecue over Direct Medium heat for 8 minutes, turning once halfway through cooking.

TIP
Resting meat not only allows the juices to settle, but the meat continues cooking during this time and the internal temperature rises to a perfect finish.

Roast Pork Tenderloin
with Plum Pickle & Hot Noodles

Gas Direct High + Indirect Medium Heat / **Weber® Q™** Direct High + Low Heat
Charcoal Indirect / **Prep time** 30 minutes + 15 minutes marinating / **Grilling time** 20 to 25 minutes / **Serves** 4

400g red plums, halved, stoned and coarsely chopped
1 cinnamon stick, halved
1 red chilli, deseeded and chopped
150g jam sugar
100ml red wine vinegar
Oil, for brushing
2 pork tenderloin fillets, each weighing about 400g
250g Chinese thick egg noodles
2 tablespoons chilli-flavoured olive oil
Salt and freshly ground black pepper

1. Cook the plums in a large pan with the cinnamon, chilli and sugar over a low heat until the sugar has dissolved. Add the vinegar, stir well and simmer for 20 minutes, or until the plums are tender and the liquid has reduced. Remove the cinnamon stick. Transfer three-quarters of the pickled plum mixture to a serving dish, cover and set aside.

2. Trim off any excess fat and the silver skin from the pork tenderloins. Make small slashes in the meat.

3. Brush the pork with oil and sear over Direct High heat for 10 minutes (turning three times). Baste the pork with the reserved plum pickle and cook for a further 25 to 30 minutes over Indirect Medium heat (or for 15 to 20 minutes over Direct Low heat on the Weber® Q™ gas grills). Continue basting the meat periodically throughout the remaining cooking time. Remove from the grill, cover with foil and leave to rest for 5 to 10 minutes.

4. Cook the noodles according to the packet instructions. Drain and toss in the chilli-flavoured oil and season to taste. Slice the pork and serve with noodles and the reserved pickled plum mixture.

Lamb Burgers
with Pimiento Salsa

Gas Direct Medium Heat / **Weber® Q™** Direct Medium Heat / **Charcoal** Direct
Prep time 25 minutes / **Grilling time** 12 to 16 minutes / **Serves** 4

500g lean minced lamb
**1 shallot, very finely
   chopped**
1 egg
**3 garlic cloves, crushed,
   divided**
**Salt and freshly ground
   black pepper**
**A few salad leaves and
   sliced tomatoes, to serve**
**4 small burger buns,
   to serve**

For the salsa:
**390g can red pimientos,
   drained and finely chopped**
**1 small mild red chilli,
   deseeded and finely
   chopped**
2 tablespoons olive oil
**Salt and freshly ground
   black pepper**

1. Mix together the minced lamb, shallot, 2 garlic cloves and seasoning in a large bowl.

2. Mould the lamb mixture by hand into four burger shapes and barbecue over Direct Medium heat for 12 to 16 minutes, turning once, or until cooked through.

3. To make the salsa, mix together the pimientos, the remaining garlic clove and chilli, then put this into a bowl with the olive oil. Add seasoning to taste.

4. Serve the burgers, together with a little salad and pimiento salsa, in a bun that has been toasted over Direct Medium heat for 1 minute.

Lamb Cutlets
with Yogurt & Cucumber Dip

Gas Direct Medium Heat / **Weber® Q™** Direct Medium Heat / **Charcoal** Direct
Prep time 25 minutes / **Grilling time** 8 to 12 minutes / **Serves** 4

12 lamb cutlets
2 garlic cloves, crushed
2 tablespoons olive oil
**2 tablespoons fresh
  chopped rosemary**
**Salt and freshly ground
  black pepper**

For the dip:
150ml plain Greek yogurt
**7.5cm piece cucumber,
  halved, deseeded
  and chopped**
**2 tablespoons fresh
  chopped mint**

1. Mix together the garlic, olive oil, rosemary and seasoning. Trim any excess fat from the cutlets and brush the oil mixture over both sides of the lamb.

2. Barbecue over Direct Medium heat for 4 to 6 minutes on each side. Remove from the grill and cover with foil for 5 to 10 minutes to allow the meat to rest and continue cooking.

3. To make the dip: tip the yogurt into a bowl, stir in the cucumber and mint, and serve with the lamb cutlets and garlic mash if desired.

TIP
Have a fresh pot of herbs – such as rosemary, thyme and chives – to hand and pick off herbs as you need them. Just before cooking lamb, for instance, put some rosemary on the barbecue for a really nice aroma.

CHAPTER FIVE

Vegetables & Vegetarian

Seared Vegetables
with Potato Rosti

Gas Direct Medium Heat / **Weber® Q™** Direct Medium Heat / **Charcoal** Direct
Prep time 10 minutes / **Grilling time** 10 to 14 minutes / **Serves** 4

1 red pepper, halved, deseeded and quartered
1 yellow pepper, halved, deseeded and quartered
1 aubergine, trimmed, halved and cut into 1cm slices
1 red onion, cut into wedges
1 bulb fennel, trimmed and cut into wedges
75ml garlic-flavoured olive oil
Salt and freshly ground black pepper
4 ready-made potato rosti
Fresh basil leaves, to garnish

1. Brush the vegetables with some of the garlic-flavoured olive oil. Arrange carefully on the grill, making sure they don't fall through, and barbecue over Direct Medium heat for 10 to 14 minutes, turning occasionally, until the vegetables are tender.

2. Remove the vegetables from the grill and put them into a large bowl. Pour over the rest of the garlic-flavoured olive oil, season and mix well.

3. Cook the ready-made rosti according to the packet instructions. Arrange the vegetables on top of the cooked rosti, drizzle with a little garlic-flavoured oil and serve garnished with fresh basil leaves.

Grilled Halloumi
with Chilli & Herbs

Gas Direct High Heat / **Weber® Q™** Direct High Heat / **Charcoal** Direct
Prep time 10 minutes + 20 minutes marinating / **Grilling time** 4 to 7 minutes / **Serves** 4

500g halloumi cheese, drained and cut into 6mm slices
100ml basil-flavoured olive oil
1 red chilli, sliced
Small bunch of fresh basil
Small bunch of fresh coriander
4 garlic and herb focaccia rolls and a green salad, to serve
Oil, for brushing

1. Place the halloumi cheese into a bowl. Pour over the basil-flavoured olive oil and add the chilli slices. Coarsely chop the basil and coriander, add to the bowl and mix well. Cover and leave to marinate for up to 20 minutes.

2. Barbecue the halloumi over Direct High heat for 4 to 6 minutes, turning once halfway through, or until golden on both sides.

3. Meanwhile, split the focaccia rolls, brush with oil and barbecue over Direct High heat for about 1 minute on each side to warm through. Put the halloumi on individual plates and serve with the flavoured olive oil, warm bread and a green salad.

TIP

Throw baps and rolls or slices of bread on the barbecue to warm through – you'll find it makes all the difference.

Warm Goat Cheese
& Spinach Panini

Gas Direct Medium Heat / **Weber® Q™** Direct Medium Heat / **Charcoal** Direct
Prep time 10 minutes / **Grilling time** 7 minutes / **Serves** 4

2 square panini rolls, halved
2 tablespoons extra-virgin olive oil, plus extra for drizzling (optional)
Freshly ground black pepper
200g round goat cheese
20g baby spinach leaves

1. Barbecue the halved panini rolls over Direct Medium heat for 2 minutes, turning halfway through. Transfer to an aluminium container suitable for barbecues.

2. Mix together the olive oil and black pepper and cut the cheese into four slices. Place a slice of cheese on each panini, drizzle with olive oil and barbecue over Direct Medium heat for 5 minutes, or until the goat cheese starts to melt.

3. Arrange the panini on plates and put the spinach on top, where the leaves will gently wilt over the warm cheese. Drizzle with a little extra olive oil, if desired.

TIP
If your goat cheese is very ripe you may need to reduce the cooking time.

Stuffed Peppers
with Lemon & Herb Couscous

Gas Direct Medium Heat / **Weber® Q™** Direct Medium Heat / **Charcoal** Direct
Prep time 20 minutes / **Grilling time** 12 to 14 minutes / **Serves** 4

200g couscous
350ml boiling vegetable stock
5 tablespoons garlic-flavoured olive oil
2 tablespoons snipped fresh chives
4 tablespoons fresh chopped coriander
10 stoned black olives, finely chopped
½ preserved lemon, finely chopped, or to taste
200g feta cheese (suitable for vegetarians), finely crumbled
Salt and freshly ground black pepper
4 red peppers

1. Put the couscous in a bowl and pour over the hot vegetable stock. Cover with clingfilm and leave to stand for 5 minutes, or until the stock is absorbed. Add 3 tablespoons of the garlic-flavoured oil, the herbs, olives, lemon and feta. Season to taste.

2. Cut the peppers in half, remove and discard the seeds and white membrane, and brush with the remaining oil. Barbecue over Direct Medium heat for 4 minutes, cut side down.

3. Remove from the grill and arrange in a Weber vegetable basket or foil container. Fill the peppers with the couscous mixture, then return to the barbecue and cook, cut side up, for a further 8 to 10 minutes, or until the peppers are tender and the couscous is hot right through.

Aubergine Strips
with Fresh Pesto

Gas Direct Medium Heat / **Weber® Q™** Direct Medium Heat / **Charcoal** Direct
Prep time 15 minutes / **Grilling time** 8 to 10 minutes / **Serves** 4

**2 large aubergines, trimmed
and cut into 1.5cm slices**

For the classic pesto:
50g fresh basil leaves
2 large garlic cloves
50g pine nuts
**50g freshly grated
Parmesan cheese**
**Salt and freshly ground
black pepper**
150ml olive oil
**A mixed green salad and
pine nuts, to serve**

1. To make the pesto, put the basil, garlic, pine nuts and Parmesan in a food processor and blend to a purée. Season and then, with the motor running, gradually add the olive oil to make a smooth, thick pesto.

2. Brush both sides of the aubergine slices with the pesto and barbecue over Direct Medium heat for 8 to 10 minutes, or until tender, turning once. Serve the hot aubergine slices with any leftover pesto, sprinkled with pine nuts and a mixed green salad.

TIP

You can also make different types of pesto instead of the classic one. Try replacing the basil with coriander leaves or for a more peppery flavour use rocket instead of the basil.

Squash
with Ginger & Chilli Dip

Gas Direct Medium Heat / **Weber® Q™** Direct Medium Heat / **Charcoal** Direct
Prep time 15 minutes / **Grilling time** 8 to 10 minutes / **Serves** 4

**2 large green courgettes,
trimmed and cut into
1.5cm slices**
**1 butternut squash, peeled,
halved, deseeded and cut
into 1.5cm slices**
8 tablespoons olive oil
**Salt and freshly ground
black pepper**

For the dip:
150ml mayonnaise
**1 teaspoon harissa, or
to taste**
**1cm piece fresh root ginger,
peeled and grated**

1. Brush the courgettes and squash with olive oil and barbecue over Direct Medium heat for 8 to 10 minutes, turning once, until tender.

2. Meanwhile, mix together the ingredients for the dip.

3. When they are ready, serve the grilled vegetables with the dip, scattered with freshly chopped herbs.

TIP
Make sure the vegetables are the same size so they will cook at the same time. You could use halved and deseeded red or orange peppers instead of the squash if you prefer. If you cook a selection of vegetables check the grilling charts on pages 22–27 for relevant cooking times.

Field Mushrooms
Oozing with Brie

Gas Direct Medium Heat / **Weber® Q™** Direct Medium Heat / **Charcoal** Direct
Prep time 5 minutes / **Grilling time** 8 to 10 minutes / **Serves** 4

4 flat field mushrooms
Light olive oil for brushing
200g Brie, cut into tiny
　cubes
4 tablespoons fresh
　chopped basil or coriander
4 tablespoons fresh white
　breadcrumbs
Salt and cayenne pepper

1. Wipe the mushrooms, remove and discard the stalks, and brush the underside with olive oil.

2. Mix together the remaining ingredients and use to fill the mushrooms.

3. Set in a Weber vegetable basket or foil container and barbecue over Direct Medium heat for 8 to 10 minutes, or until the mushrooms are tender when pierced with a knife and the cheese is oozing.

TIP
Remember that a change in weather can affect your barbecue times. Allow a little more cooking time on colder days and less cooking time in extreme hot weather.

Marinated Tofu Slices

Gas Direct High Heat / **Weber® Q™** Direct High Heat / **Charcoal** Direct
Prep time 10 minutes + 1 hour marinating / **Grilling time** 2 to 4 minutes / **Serves** 4

600g tofu, drained weight, cut into 1cm slices
Fresh chopped coriander, to garnish

For the marinade:
1 garlic clove, crushed
1 red chilli, deseeded and chopped
4 tablespoons sesame oil
2 tablespoons white wine vinegar
8 tablespoons dark soy sauce
1 small red onion, finely chopped

1. Arrange the tofu slices in a single layer in a non-metallic dish. Mix together the ingredients for the marinade and pour over the tofu slices. Cover and chill for 1 hour, turning once.

2. Remove the tofu slices and discard the marinade. Barbecue over Direct High heat for 2 to 4 minutes, turning once.

3. Serve garnished with the coriander.

TIP
Always wash your hands, chopping board and knife thoroughly after preparing the chilli for the marinade as the volatile oils can cause irritation. Avoid touching your eyes, nose and mouth until you have washed your hands. If necessary wear rubber gloves.

CHAPTER SIX

Desserts

Seared Peaches
with Vanilla Syrup & Fresh Raspberries

Gas Direct Medium Heat / **Weber® Q™** Direct Medium Heat / **Charcoal** Direct
Prep time 5 minutes / **Grilling time** 3 to 4 minutes / **Serves** 4

**6 ripe peaches or
   nectarines
2 teaspoons gourmet vanilla
   syrup or golden syrup,
   plus a little extra
   (optional)
1 tablespoon clear honey
1 tablespoon oil
150g crème fraîche
200g fresh raspberries
Fresh mint sprigs, to
   garnish**

1. Cut the peaches in half and remove the stones. Mix the vanilla or golden syrup, honey and oil together in a small bowl and drizzle this over the peach halves.

2. Barbecue the peaches over Direct Medium heat for 3 to 4 minutes, turning once, to sear the fruit.

3. Put the crème fraîche in a bowl and stir in the raspberries (reserve a few to use as a garnish).

4. Serve the cool raspberry crème fraîche with the hot fruit, a little extra vanilla syrup, the reserved raspberries and some mint sprigs, if desired.

TIP

Experiment with different flavours according to which fruits are in season.

Sizzling Strawberries
with Chocolate Dip

Gas Indirect Medium Heat / **Weber® Q™** Direct Low Heat / **Charcoal** Indirect
Prep time 15 minutes / **Grilling time** 6 minutes / **Serves** 6

350ml double cream
3 tablespoons Grand Marnier
200g good-quality plain dark chocolate, chopped
600g large, firm strawberries, hulled
1 to 2 tablespoons icing sugar

1. Put the cream, liqueur and chocolate into a heavy-based pan and heat gently, stirring, until the chocolate is melted and you have a lovely thick, glossy sauce. Remove from the heat and leave to stand while barbecuing the strawberries (this gives the sauce time to thicken so it will coat the strawberries perfectly).

2. Dust the strawberries with icing sugar, then, cooking in batches, carefully arrange them on the grill so they don't fall through. Barbecue over Indirect Medium heat (or Direct Low heat on the Weber® Q™ gas grills) for 6 minutes, turning once halfway through (they shouldn't be too soft).

3. Pour a little chocolate sauce into individual dishes (ramekins are ideal). For dipping, serve the strawberries pierced with cocktail sticks.

TIP
If you are serving this dessert to children, remember to omit the Grand Marnier from the chocolate mixture.

Marsala-soaked Figs
with Mascarpone

Gas Direct Medium Heat / **Weber® Q™** Direct Medium Heat / **Charcoal** Direct
Prep time 5 minutes + 5 minutes soaking / **Grilling time** 4 minutes / **Serves** 4

8 fresh figs, halved
4 tablespoons Marsala
4 tablespoons mascarpone
1 tablespoon icing sugar, or
 to taste
A few drops of vanilla
 extract

1. Put the figs in a dish and drizzle with Marsala. Leave to stand for 5 minutes to allow the fortified wine to soak through the figs.

2. Mix together the mascarpone, icing sugar and vanilla extract in a bowl.

3. Barbecue the marsala-soaked figs over Direct Medium heat, cut-side down first, for 4 minutes. Turn once halfway through cooking.

4. Remove from the grill and serve hot with the flavoured mascarpone.

TIP
Try ricotta cheese, double cream or even plain Greek yogurt in place of the mascarpone cheese if you prefer.

Hot & Spicy Fruit Salad

Gas Direct Medium Heat / **Weber® Q™** Direct Medium Heat / **Charcoal** Direct
Prep time 15 minutes / **Grilling time** 10 to 15 minutes / **Serves** 4

75g butter
½ to 1 teaspoon garam masala
1 tablespoon icing sugar
2 bananas, peeled and cut into chunks
2 plums, stoned and quartered
2 nectarines, stoned and cut into chunks
200g fresh pineapple chunks
Vanilla ice cream, to serve

1. Melt the butter, garam masala and icing sugar in a large aluminium container suitable for use on the barbecue over Direct Medium heat.

2. Add the prepared fruit, toss well in the spiced butter and grill for 10 to 15 minutes, stirring and turning once.

3. Divide the hot fruit salad between four dishes and serve with a scoop of vanilla ice cream.

TIP

Other fruit will also work well for this recipe. Try peaches, apples, pears and even mango chunks.